budgetbooks

CLASSIC ROCK

ISBN 0-634-04858-9

7777 W. BLUEMOUND RD. P.O. BOX 13819 MILWAUKEE, WI 53213

Visit Hal Leonard Online at
www.halleonard.com

CONTENTS

AGAINST ALL ODDS
(Take a Look at Me Now)

Words and Music by
PHIL COLLINS

Original key: Db major. This edition has been transposed down one half-step to be more playable.

AUTHORITY SONG

Words and Music by
JOHN MELLENCAMP

BACK IN THE U.S.S.R.

Words and Music by JOHN LENNON
and PAUL McCARTNEY

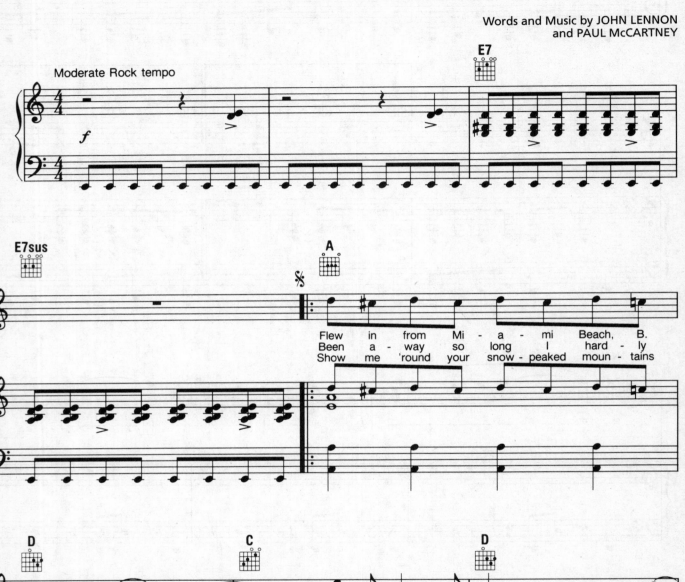

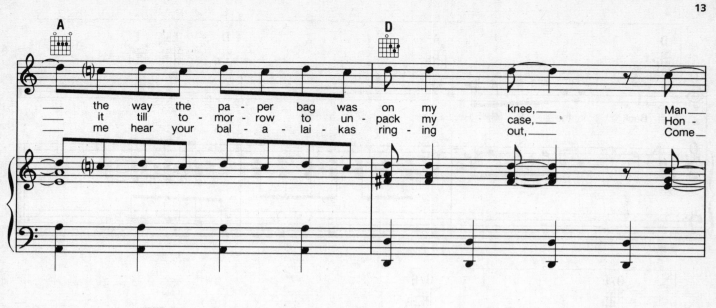

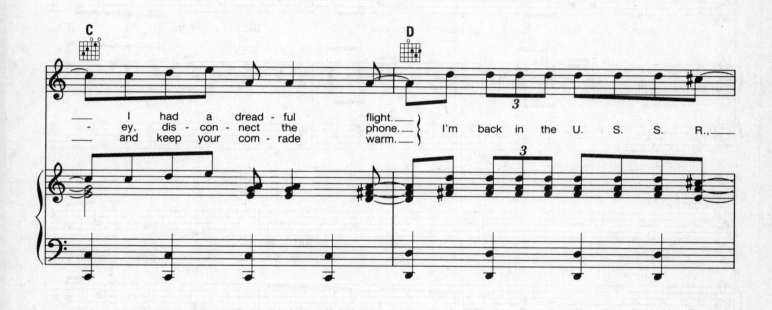

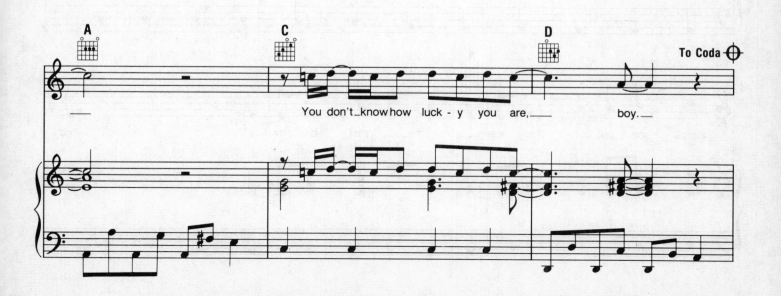

BADGE

Words and Music by ERIC CLAPTON
and GEORGE HARRISON

Think-in' 'bout the times you drove __ in my car. __
I told you not to wan - der 'round __ in the dark. __
Talk - in' 'bout a girl that looks __ quite like you. __

Think-in' that I might have drove __ you too far. __
I told you 'bout the swans that they live in the park. __
She did - n't have the time to wait __ in the queue. __

And I'm think-in' 'bout the
Then I told you 'bout the
She cried a - way her

BALLROOM BLITZ

Words and Music by MIKE CHAPMAN
and NICKY CHINN

Oh, it's been get-ting so ___ hard, liv-ing with ___ the things ___ you do ___ to me.

I'm reach-ing out for some- thing; touch-ing noth- ing's all ___ I ev- er do. ___

BEST OF MY LOVE

Words and Music by JOHN DAVID SOUTHER,
DON HENLEY and GLENN FREY

be all right if I could go on sleep - ing. But

ev - 'ry morn - in' I wake up and wor - ry

what's gon-na hap-pen to-day; you see it your way, and

I see it mine, but we both see it slip-pin' a-way.

BETH

Words and Music by PETER CRISS, BOB EZRIN
and STAN PENRIDGE

Rock Ballad, with feeling

Beth, I hear __ you call - in', but I can't come home right now. __
You say you feel __ so emp - ty, that our house just ain't a home. __

Me and the boys __ are play - in' and we just can't find the sound. __
I'm al - ways some - where else __ and __ you're al - ways there a - lone. __

BOHEMIAN RHAPSODY

Words and Music by
FREDDIE MERCURY

CALL ME THE BREEZE

Words and Music by
JOHN CALE

44

changes in me   And I ain't
hidin' from nobody,   nobody's hidin' from me.

1 This may be repeated ad lib. for instr.   2,3 (To Verses)   4 D. S. al Fine

2. I got that   They

ADDITIONAL LYRICS

Verse 2.
Well, I got that green light, baby
I got to keep movin' on
Well, I got that green light, baby
I got to keep movin' on
Well I might go out to California
Might go down to Georgia, I don't know.

Verse 3.
Well, I dig you Georgia peaches
Makes me feel right at home
Well, I dig you Georgia peaches
Makes me feel right at home
But I don't love me no one woman
So I can't stay in Georgia long.

CAUGHT UP IN YOU

Words and Music by FRANK SULLIVAN, JIM PETERIK,
JEFF CARLISI and DON BARNES

D.S. (lyric 2) and Fade

COME TOGETHER

Words and Music by JOHN LENNON
and PAUL McCARTNEY

Moderately slow, with a double-time feeling

Here come old flat-top, He come groov-ing up slow-ly, He got Joo Joo eye-ball, He one ho-ly roll-er, He got hair down to his knee.

Got to be a jok-er, He just do what he please.

He wear no shoe-shine, He got
He Bag Pro - duc - tion, He got
He roll - er coast - er, He got

toe - jam foot-ball, He got mon - key fin-ger, He shoot Co - ca Co - la, He say,
wal - rus gum-boot, He got O - no side-board, He one spi - nal crack-er, He got
ear - ly warn-ing, He got Mud - dy Wa - ter, He one Mo - jo fil-ter, He say,

"I know_ you, you know me."_
feet down be - low___ his knee.___
"One and one and one___ is three.".

One thing I can tell you is you
Hold you in his arm-chair, you can
Got to be good look-ing 'cause he

COME SAIL AWAY

Words and Music by
DENNIS DeYOUNG

56

DAY TRIPPER

Words and Music by JOHN LENNON
and PAUL McCARTNEY

E7

Got a good rea - son
She's a big tea - ser,
Tried to please_ her,

for

It took me so_____ long_____ to find out,—
It took me so_____ long_____ to find out,—
It took me so_____ long_____ to find out,—

and I found out.
and I found
and I found out.

no chord

Ah_____

cresc.

DON'T DO ME LIKE THAT

Words and Music by
TOM PETTY

(1.) I was talk - in' with a friend of mine,   said a wom - an had   hurt his pride.

(2., D.S.)   Lis - ten hon - ey, can you see?   Ba - by, it would bur - y me

DON'T FEAR THE REAPER

Words and Music by
DONALD ROESER

Sea - sons don't fear the reap - er, nor do the wind, the sun or the rain. __

__ (We can be like they __ are.) Come on, ba - by. (Don't fear the reap -

- er.) Ba - by, take my hand. __ (Don't fear the reap - er.) We'll be a - ble to fly. __

__ (Don't fear the reap - er.) Ba - by, I'm your man. ____

DON'T LET THE SUN GO DOWN ON ME

Words and Music by ELTON JOHN
and BERNIE TAUPIN

I can't_ light

no more of your dark -

- ness.

All my pic - tures _____ seem to fade_ to black_ and white. _

DON'T STAND SO CLOSE TO ME

Written and Composed by
STING

DON'T STOP

Words and Music by
CHRISTINE McVIE

DREAM ON

Words and Music by
STEVEN TYLER

Repeat and Fade

DREAMER

Words and Music by RICK DAVIES
and ROGER HODGSON

100

I'll take a life, take a hol - i - day.

Take a lie, take a dream - er.

Dream, (dream,) dream, (dream,) dream, (dream,) dream, dream a - long...

DRIVE MY CAR

Words and Music by JOHN LENNON
and PAUL McCARTNEY

Ba- by, you can drive my car, ___ Yes, I'm gon- na be a star, ___

Ba- by, you can drive my car, ___ and may- be I'll love ___ you.''

D.S. al Coda

CODA

Repeat and Fade

Beep, beep, mm beep, beep. Yeah. ___

EYE IN THE SKY

Words and Music by ALAN PARSONS
and ERIC WOOLFSON

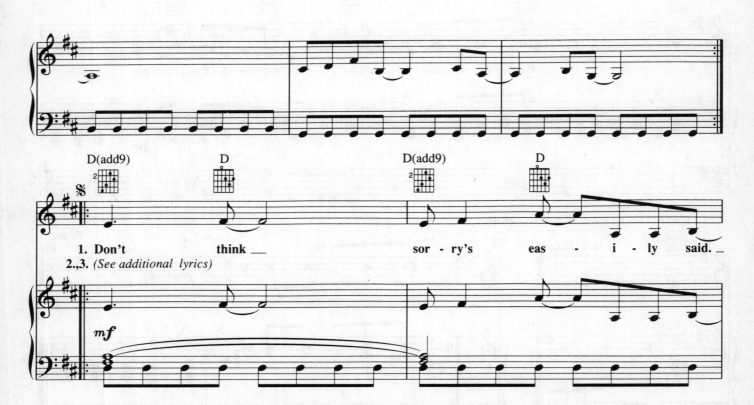

1. Don't think _____ sor - ry's eas - i - ly said. _____
2.,3. (See additional lyrics)

Additional Lyrics

2. Don't say words you're gonna regret.
   Don't let the fire rush to your head.
   I've heard the accusation before,
   And I ain't gonna take any more,
   Believe me.
   The sun in your eyes
   Made some of the lies worth believing.
   (To Chorus:)

3. Don't leave false illusions behind.
   Don't cry 'cause I ain't changing my mind.
   So find another fool like before,
   'Cause I ain't gonna live anymore believing
   Some of the lies, while all of the signs are deceiving.
   (To Chorus:)

GIVE A LITTLE BIT

Words and Music by RICK DAVIES
and ROGER HODGSON

FAITHFULLY

Words and Music by
JONATHAN CAIN

1. High - way,

run in - to the mid - night sun.

2. (See additional lyrics)

Wheels go 'round and 'round; you're on my mind.

1. Oh, _____
2. 3. 4. 5. *(Vocal ad lib.)*

oh _____

oh. _____

Verse 2:
Circus life
Under the big top world;
We all need the clowns
To make us smile.
Through space and time
Always another show.
Wondering where I am;
Lost without you.

And being apart ain't easy
On this love affair;
Two strangers learn to fall
In love again.
I get the joy
Of rediscovering you.
Oh girl, you stand by me.
I'm forever yours, faithfully.

FREE RIDE

Words and Music by
DAN HARTMAN

Come on ___ and take a free ride.

All Yeah, yeah, yeah, yeah.

GLORIA

Words and Music by
VAN MORRISON

Steady Rock

Like to tell you 'bout my ba - by.
here,
You know she___ comes 'round___
just a - bout___ mid - night.___

___
Makes me feel so
just 'bout five feet
good Lord,
four___
from her head to the
makes me feel___ al -

ground.___
right.___
Well, she comes a - round here___
Walk - in down my street,___
just a - bout mid -
comes up to my

GREEN-EYED LADY

Words and Music by JERRY CORBETTA,
J.C. PHILLIPS and DAVID RIORDAN

132

HEART AND SOUL

Words and Music by MIKE CHAPMAN
and NICKY CHINN

HEROES

Words by DAVID BOWIE
Music by DAVID BOWIE and BRIAN ENO

HEAT OF THE MOMENT

Words and Music by GEOFFREY DOWNES
and JOHN WETTON

HEAVEN

Words and Music by BRYAN ADAMS
and JIM VALLANCE

HIGHER LOVE

Words and Music by WILL JENNINGS
and STEVE WINWOOD

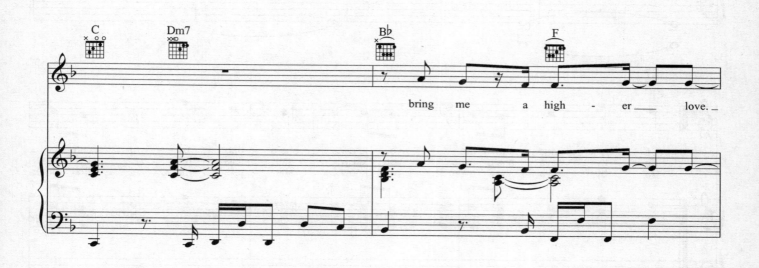

I FEEL FINE

Words and Music by JOHN LENNON
and PAUL McCARTNEY

IF YOU LEAVE ME NOW

Words and Music by
PETER CETERA

- row comes, ___ then we'll both ___ re - gret ___ the things we said ___ to - day. ___

173

I WANT TO KNOW WHAT LOVE IS

Words and Music by
MICK JONES

I WANT YOU TO WANT ME

Words and Music by
RICK NIELSEN

Bright Two-Beat

I want you to want ___ me.

I need you to need ___ me.

I'd

180

IT'S ONLY LOVE

Words and Music by BRYAN ADAMS
and JIM VALLANCE

When the feel-in' is end-ed, there ain't
heart has been bro-ken, hard
shat-tered, _____ ain't _____

no use pre-tend-in'. Don't ya wor-ry, Well, it's on-ly love. When your
words have been spo-ken, it ain't eas-y, but it's on-ly love. And if your
noth-in' else mat-ters. It ain't o-ver, it's _____ on-ly love. If your

You can live with-out the ag - gra - va - tion.

Ya got - ta wan - na win. _

Ya got - ta wan - na win. _

You keep look - in' back in des - per - a - tion

o - ver _ and o - ver _ and o - ver a - gain.

MAGGIE MAY

Words and Music by ROD STEWART
and MARTIN QUITTENTON

Additional Lyrics

2. You lured me away from home, just to save you from being alone.
You stole my soul, that's a pain I can do without.
All I needed was a friend to lend a guiding hand.
But you turned into a lover, and, Mother, what a lover! You wore me out.
All you did was wreck my bed and in the morning kick me in the head.
Oh, Maggie, I couldn't have tried any more.

3. You lured me away from home 'cause you didn't want to be alone.
You stole my heart, I couldn't leave you if I tried.
I suppose I could collect my books and get back to school,
Or steal my Daddy's cue and make a living out of playing pool,
Or find myself a rock and roll band that needs a helpin' hand.
Oh, Maggie, I wish I'd never seen your face. *(To Coda)*

MELISSA

Words and Music by GREGG ALLMAN
and STEVE ALAIMO

MONEY

Words and Music by
ROGER WATERS

Mon - ey,   ya get a - way.   Ya get a
Mon - ey,   you get back.   I'm
Mon - ey,   it's a crime.   Share it

good job with more pay, and you're O._____ K.
all right, with Jack. Keep your hands off my_____ stack.
fair - ly, but don't take a slice of my_____ pie.

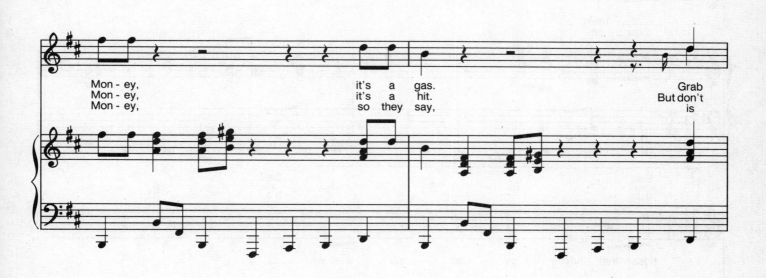

Mon - ey,_____ it's a gas._____ Grab
Mon - ey,_____ it's a hit._____ But don't
Mon - ey,_____ so they say,_____ is

that cash with both hands and make____ a stash._____ I'm in the
give me that do - good - y good bull - shit._____ But if
the root of all e - vil to - day.

NEW KID IN TOWN

Words and Music by JOHN DAVID SOUTHER,
DON HENLEY and GLENN FREY

There's talk on the street;__ it sounds so fa - mil - iar.
You look in her eyes;__ the mu - sic be - gins to play.

John-ny-come-late - ly, the new kid in town.
John-ny-come-late - ly, the new kid in town.

Ev-'ry-bod- y loves — you, so don't_ let them down._
Will she still love — you

when you're not a - round?_____

There's so man-y things you should have told — her,

OWNER OF A LONELY HEART

Words and Music by TREVOR HORN, JON ANDERSON,
TREVOR RABIN and CHRIS SQUIRE

Own - er of a lone - ly heart.

PAPERBACK WRITER

Words and Music by JOHN LENNON
and PAUL McCARTNEY

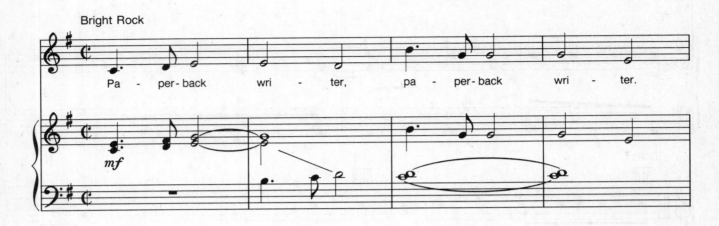

PENNY LANE

Words and Music by JOHN LENNON
and PAUL McCARTNEY

219

PHILADELPHIA FREEDOM

Words and Music by ELTON JOHN
and BERNIE TAUPIN

Additional Lyrics

2. If you choose to, you can live your life alone.
   Some people choose the city,
   Some others choose the good old family home.
   I like living easy without family ties,
   'Til the whippoorwill of freedom zapped me
   Right between the eyes.

Repeat Chorus

PICTURES OF LILY

Words and Music by
PETER TOWNSHEND

PINK HOUSES

Words and Music by
JOHN MELLENCAMP

There's a   black man
young man
peo - ple   with a   black   cat
in a   T - shirt
and more peo - ple.

liv - in' in   a   black neigh - bor - hood. _____   He's   got   an
lis - t'nin' to   a   rock - in' roll - in'   sta - tion. ____   He's   got
What   do   they   know? _____

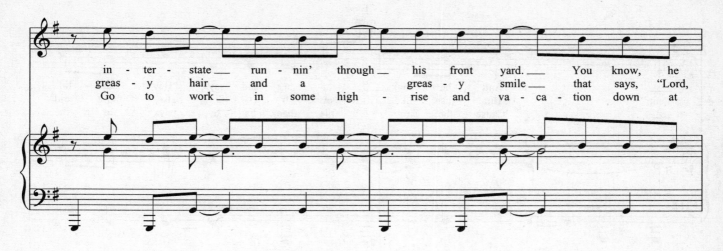

in - ter - state __ run - nin' through __ his front yard. __ You know, he
greas - y hair __ and a greas - y smile __ that says, "Lord,
Go to work __ in some high - rise and va - ca - tion down at

F   C   G

thinks he's got it so good. __ And there's a
this must be my des - ti - na - tion." 'Cause they
the Gulf of Mex - i - co. __ And there's

wom - an in the kitch - en clean - in' up the eve - nin' slop. __
told me when I was young - er, "Boy, you gon - na be Pres - i -
win - ners and there's los - ers, but they ain't no big deal. __

RADAR LOVE

Words and Music by GEORGE KOOYMANS
and BARRY HAY

I've been driv - in' all night. My hand's wet on the wheel.
ra - di - o was play-in' some for - got - ten song. _
No more speed, I'm al - most there.

There's a voice _ in my head _ that
Bren - da Lee _ is
I got - ta keep cool now, I

drives   my   heel. ___   It's my ba -
com - in' on   strong. ___   The road _
got - ta take   care. ___   Last _

___ by call - in', said, "I need ___ you here." _
___ com - in' car to pass,   here ___ I go. ___
___ has got ___ me hyp - no - tized. _

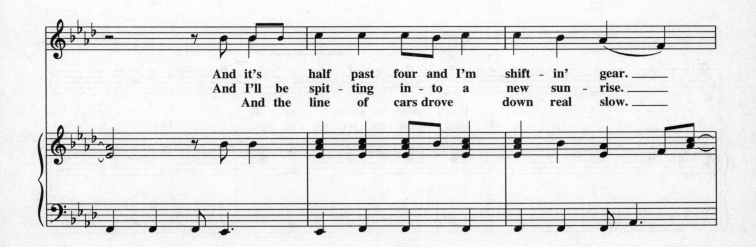

And it's   half past four and I'm   shift - in'   gear. _____
And I'll be   spit - ting   in - to a   new   sun - rise. _____
And the   line of cars drove   down real   slow. _____

241

that's   called _____   ra - dar   love. _

RENEGADE

Words and Music by
TOMMY SHAW

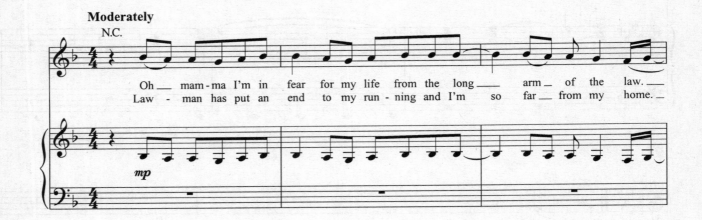

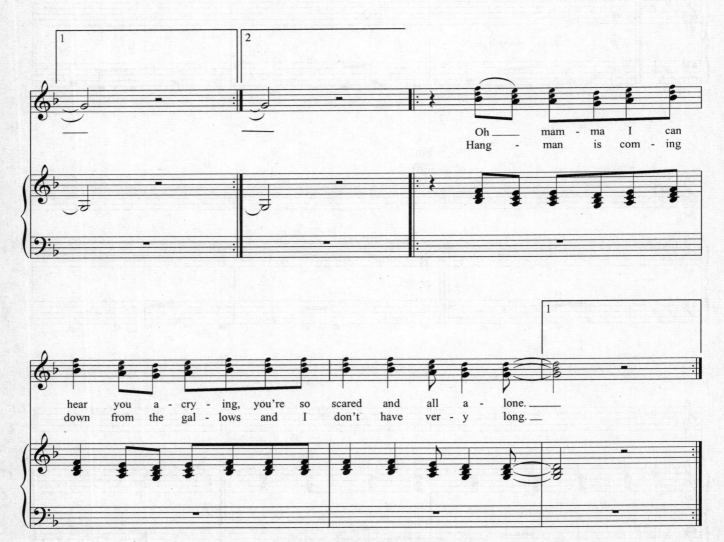

scared and all a - lone.

Hang - man is com - ing down from the gal - lows and I don't

D.S. al Coda

have ver - y long. The

CODA

N.C.

Ad lib. Guitar

RHIANNON

Words and Music by
STEVIE NICKS

Rhi - an - non rings___ like a bell through the night, and
She is ___ like a cat in the dark, and

would-n't you love to love ___ her? ___
then she is the dark - ness. ___

Takes to the sky like a
She rules her life like a

bird   in   flight, ___   and   who   will   be ___   her   lov -
fine   sky - lark ___   and   when   the   sky ___   is

- er? }
star - less. }   All   your   life ___   you've   nev - er   seen   a   wom-an ___

___   tak - en   by   the   wind. ___   Would   you   stay ___   if   she   prom -

ROXANNE

Written and Composed by
STING

RUNNING ON FAITH

Words and Music by
JERRY WILLIAMS

Late-ly, I've been run-nin' on _____ faith. _____
Late-ly, I've been talk - in' in _____ my sleep.

SHAKEDOWN
from the Paramount Motion Picture BEVERLY HILLS COP II

Words and Music by KEITH FORSEY,
HAROLD FALTERMEYER and BOB SEGER

This is the

Shake-down, break down, take-down; eve-

-ry-bod-y wants in-to the crowd-ed light.

SHOW ME THE WAY

Words and Music by
PETER FRAMPTON

I won-der how__ you're feel-ing.__ There's
I can see__ no rea-son.__ You're

I watch you when you're sleep - ing; well then I

want to take your love. Oh, won't you

show me the way, ev - 'ry day? I want you;

show me the way. One more time! I want

(She's)
SOME KIND OF WONDERFUL

Words and Music by
JOHN ELLISON

I don't need ____ a whole lot's of mon - ey. ____ her in my arms ____ I don't need ___ you know she

____ a big fine car. I got ev - 'ry - thing ___ that __ a
sets my soul on fire. Ooh ___ when my ba - by kiss -

man could want. I got more____ than I could ask___
es me my heart be-comes filled___ with de-

___ for. I, I don't___ have to
sire.___ When she wraps her lov-in' arms___ a-round___

run a-round. I don't have___ to stay out all night.
__ me it 'bout drives me out of my mind.___

'Cause I got me a sweet a sweet lov - in'
Yeah, when my ba - by kiss -

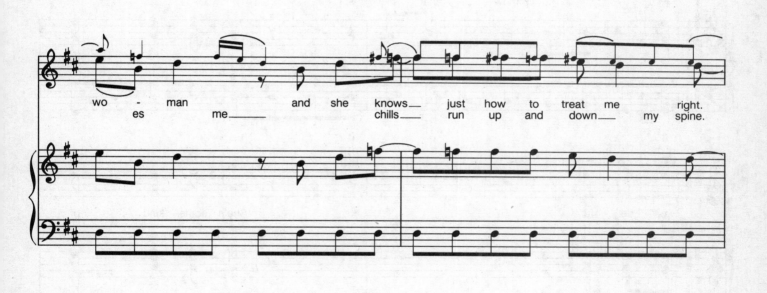

wo - man and she knows just how to treat me right.
es me chills run up and down my spine.

Well my ba - by, she's al - right.

SUMMER OF '69

Words and Music by BRYAN ADAMS
and JIM VALLANCE

THIRTY DAYS IN THE HOLE

Words and Music by
STEVE MARRIOTT

SWEET EMOTION

Words and Music by STEVEN TYLER
and TOM HAMILTON

You're call - in' my name but I
Well, I got good news, she's a
You're tell - in' her things but your
I'm talk - in' 'bout some - thin' you can

got - ta make clear. _____
real good li - ar, _____
girl - friend lied; _____
sure un - der - stand, _____

I
'cause my
you
'cause a

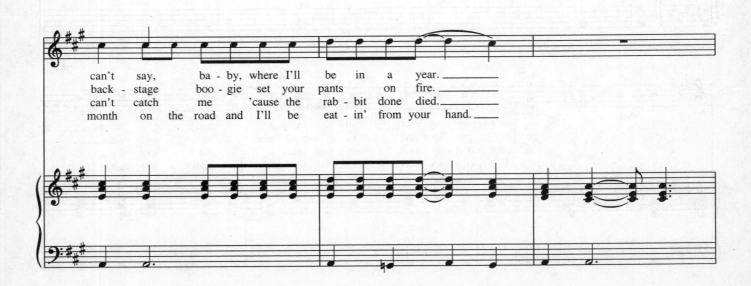

can't say, ba - by, where I'll be in a year. _____
back - stage boo - gie set your pants on fire. _____
can't catch me 'cause the rab - bit done died. _____
month on the road and I'll be eat - in' from your hand. _____

TAKIN' CARE OF BUSINESS

Words and Music by
RANDY BACHMAN

city.
mel - low.

There's a whis - tle up a - bove and peo - ple
Get a sec - ond hand gui - tar_____ chanc - es

push - in', peo - ple shov - in' and the girls who try to look
are you'll go_____ far. If you get in with the right bunch of fel -

pret - ty.
lows.

And if your train's on time, you can
Peo - ple see you hav - in' fun, just a

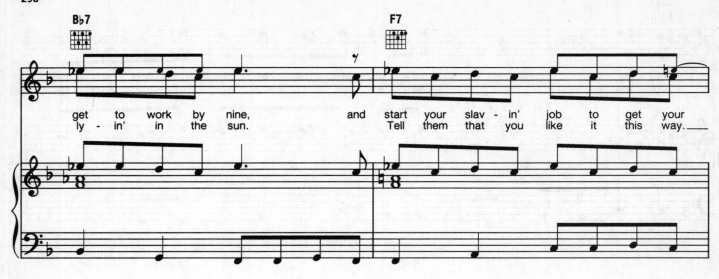

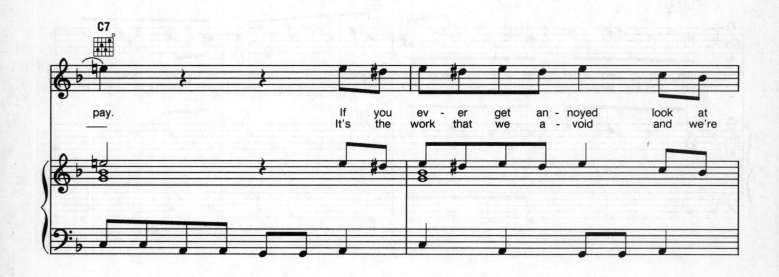

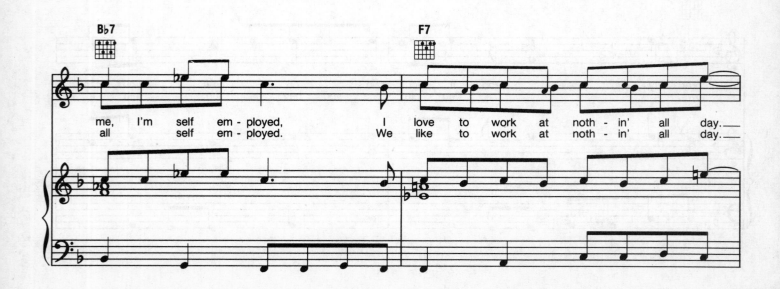

work-in' o - ver - time, work - out.
work-in' o - ver - time.

There's work

THESE EYES

Written by BURTON CUMMINGS
and RANDY BACHMAN

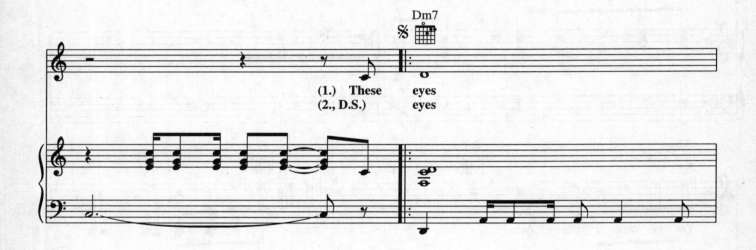

(1.) These   eyes
(2., D.S.)   eyes

cry   ev - 'ry   night   for   you.   These
watched you bring my world   to an   end.   This

THROWING IT ALL AWAY

Words and Music by TONY BANKS,
PHIL COLLINS and MIKE RUTHERFORD

Need I say I love you need I say I care
can-not live to-geth-er we cannot live a-part
Someday you'll be sor-ry someday when you're free

need I say that e-mo-tion's something we don't share
that's the sit-u-a-tion I've known it from the start
memories will re-mind you that our love was meant to be

WILD THING

Words and Music by
CHIP TAYLOR

TIME FOR ME TO FLY

Words and Music by
KEVIN CRONIN

TWO OUT OF THREE AIN'T BAD

Words and Music by
JIM STEINMAN

WALK OF LIFE

Words and Music by
MARK KNOPFLER

WALK ON THE WILD SIDE

Words and Music by
LOU REED

WE ARE THE CHAMPIONS

Words and Music by
FREDDIE MERCURY

WORKING FOR THE WEEKEND

Words and Music by PAUL DEAN,
MATTHEW FRENETTE and MICHAEL RENO

YOU GIVE LOVE A BAD NAME

Words and Music by DESMOND CHILD,
JON BON JOVI and RICHIE SAMBORA

Medium Rock

Shot through the heart ___ and you're to ___ blame. Dar-lin', you give love ___ a

bad name.

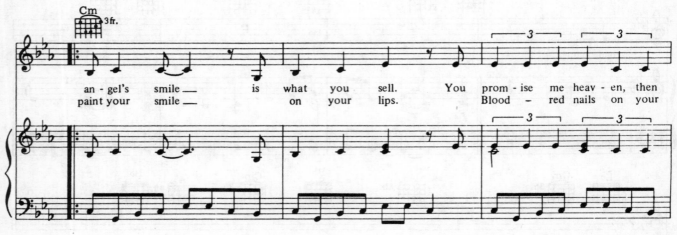

an - gel's smile ___ is what you sell. You prom - ise me heav - en, then
paint your smile ___ on your lips. Blood — red nails on your

put me through hell. Chains of ___ love ___ got a hold on me. When
fin - ger - tips. A school boy's ___ dream, ___ you act so shy. Your

YOU REALLY GOT ME

Words and Music by
RAY DAVIES

1. Girl you real-ly got me go-ing you got me
2. See don't ev-er set me free I al-ways
3. See don't ev-er set me free I al-ways

so I don't know what I'm do-ing
wan-na be by your side
wan-na be by your side

Yeah
Girl } you real-ly got me now You got me
Girl